Reproduction of Copyrighted Works By Educators and Librarians

Library of Congress. Copyright Office.

Many educators and librarians ask about the fair use and photocopying provisions of the copyright law. The Copyright Office cannot give legal advice or offer opinions on what is permitted or prohibited. However, we have published in this circular basic information on some of the most important legislative provisions and other documents dealing with reproduction by librarians and educators.

Also available is the 1983 Report of the Register of Copyrights on Library Reproduction of Copyrighted Works (17 U.S.C. 108). The Report and seven appendixes can be purchased in microfiche or paper copies by written request from the National Technical Information Service, U.S. Department of Commerce, 5285 Port Royal Road, Springfield, VA 22161 or by calling the Sales Desk at (703)487-4650. The FAX number for placing orders is (703) 321-8547. The TTY number for placing orders is (703) 487-4639. When ordering, please include the fol-lowing NTIS Accession Numbers: PB83 148239ACY, Entire Set; PB83 148247ACY, Report Only; PB83 148254ACY, Appendix l (King Report); PB83 148262ACY, Appendix II (Chicago Hearing and Written Comments); PB83 148270ACY, Appendix III (Houston Hearing and Written Comments); PB83 148288ACY, Appendix IV (Washington Hearing and Written Comments); PB83 148296ACY, Appendix V (Anaheim Hearing and Written Comments); PB83 148304ACY, Appendix VI (New York Hearing and Written Comments); and PB83 148312ACY, Appendix VII (Final Written Comments).

The 1988 5-year Report of the Register of Copyrights on Library Reproduction of Copyrighted Works is also available from NTIS. Use NTIS Accession Number PB88 212014ACY.

CONTENTS

The Subjects Covered in This Booklet

The documentary materials collected in this booklet deal with
reproduction of copyrighted works by educators, librarians, and
archivists for a variety of uses, including:
  + Reproduction for teaching in educational institutions at all levels;
    and
  + Reproduction by libraries and archives for purposes of study,
    research, interlibrary exchanges, and archival preservation.
The documents reprinted here are limited to materials dealing with
reproduction. Under the copyright law, reproduction can take either of
two forms:
  + The making of copies: by photocopying, making micro-form
    reproductions, videotaping, or any other method of duplicating
    visually-perceptible material; and
  + The making of phonorecords: by duplicating sound recordings, taping
    off the air, or any other method of recapturing sounds.
The copyright law also contains various provisions dealing with importations, performances,
and displays of copyrighted works for educational and other noncommercial purposes, but
they are outside the scope of this booklet. You can obtain a copy of the statute and
information about specific provisions by writing to the Publications Section, LM-455,
Copyright Office, Library of Congress, Washington, D.C. 20559-6000.

A Note on the Documents Reprinted

The documentary materials in this booklet are reprints or excerpts from six sources:

1. The Copyright Act of October 19, 1976. This is the copyright law of the United States,
effective January 1, 1978 (title 17 of the United States Code, Public Law 94-553, 90 Stat.
2541).

2. The Senate Report. This is the 1975 report of the Senate Judiciary
Committee on S. 22, the Senate version of the bill that became the
Copyright Act of 1976 (S. Rep. No. 94-473, 94th Cong., 1st Sess.,
November 20 (legislative day November 18,1975)).
3. The House Report. This is the 1976 report of the House of Representatives Judiciary
Committee on the House amendments to the bill that became the Copyright Act of 1976
(H.R. Rep. No. 94-1476, 94th Cong., 2d Sess., Sep-tember 3,1976).

4. The Conference Report. This is the 1976 report of the "committee of conference on the
disagreeing votes of the two Houses on the amendments of the House to the bill (S. 22) for
the general revision of the Copyright Law" (H.R. Rep. No. 94-1733, 94th Cong., 2d Sess.,
September 29,1976).

5. The Congressional Debates. This booklet contains excerpts from the Congressional
Record of September 22, 1976, reflecting statements on the floor of Congress at the time the
bill was passed by the House of Representatives (122 CONG. REC. H 10874-76, daily
edition, September 22,1976).

6. Copyright Office Regulations. These are regulations issued by the Copyright Office under section 108 dealing with warnings of copyright for use by libraries and archives (37 Code of Federal Regulations Sec. 201.14).

Items 2 and 3 on this list—the 1975 Senate Report and the 1976 House Report—present special problems. On many points the language of these two reports is identical or closely similiar. However, the two reports were written at different times, by committees of different Houses of Congress, on somewhat different bills. As a result, the discussions on some provisions of the bills vary widely, and on certain points they disagree.

The disagreements between the Senate and House versions of the bill itself were, of course, resolved when the Act of 1976 was finally passed. However, many of the disagreements as to matters of interpretation between statements in the 1975 Senate Report and in the 1976 House Report were left partly or wholly unresolved. It is therefore difficult in compiling a booklet such as this to decide in some cases what to include and what to leave out.

The House Report was written later than the Senate Report, and in many cases it adopted the language of the Senate Report, updating it and conforming it to the version of the bill that was finally enacted into law. Thus, where the differences between the two Reports are relatively minor, or where the discussion in the House Report appears to have superseded the discussion of the same point in the Senate Report, we have used the House Report as the source of our documentation. In other cases we have included excerpts from both discussions in an effort to present the legislative history as fully and fairly as possible. Anyone making a thorough study of the Act of 1976 as it affects librarians and educators should not, of course, rely exclusively on the excerpts reprinted here but should go back to the primary documentary sources.

———————— B. EXCLUSIVE RIGHTS IN COPYRIGHTED WORKS ————————

1. Text of Section 106

==
The following is a reprint of the entire text of section 106 of title 17, United States Code.
==

Section 106. Exclusive rights in copyrighted works

Subject to sections 107 through 120, the owner of copyright under this title has the exclusive rights to do and to authorize any of the following: (1) to reproduce the copyrighted work in copies or phonorecords; (2) to prepare derivative works based upon the copyrighted work; (3) to distribute copies or phonorecords of the copyrighted work to the public by sale or other transfer of ownership, or by rental, lease, or lending; (4) in the case of literary, musical, dramatic, and choreographic works, pantomimes, and motion pictures and other audiovisual works, to perform the copyrighted work publicly; and (5) in the case of literary, musical, dramatic, and choreographic works, pantomimes, and pictorial, graphic, or sculptural works, including the individual images of a motion picture or other audiovisual work, to display the copyrighted work publicly.

2. Excerpts From House Report on Section 106

==

The following excerpts are reprinted from the House Report on the new copyright law (H.R. Rep. No. 94-1476, pages 61-62). The text of the corresponding Senate Report (S. Rep. No. 94-473, pages 57-58) is substantially the same.

==

SECTION 106. EXCLUSIVE RIGHTS IN COPYRIGHTED WORKS
General scope of copyright

The five fundamental rights that the bill gives to copyright owners—the exclusive rights of reproduction, adaptation, publication, performance, and display—are stated generally in section 106. These exclusive rights, which comprise the so-called "bundle of rights" that is a copyright, are cumulative and may overlap in some cases. Each of the five enumerated rights may be subdivided indefinitely and, as discussed below in connection with section 201, each subdivision of an exclusive right may be owned and enforced separately.

The approach of the bill is to set forth the copyright owner's exclusive rights in broad terms in section 106, and then to provide various limitations, qualifications, or exemptions in the 12 sections that follow. Thus, everything in section 106 is made "subject to sections 107 through 118," and must be read in conjunction with those provisions.

* * *

Rights of reproduction, adaptation, and publication

The first three clauses of section 106, which cover all rights under a copyright except those of performance and display, extend to every kind of copyrighted work. The exclusive rights encompassed by these clauses, though closely related, are independent; they can generally be characterized as rights of copying, recording, adaptation, and publishing. A single act of infringement may violate all of these rights at once, as where a publisher reproduces, adapts, and sells copies of a person's copyrighted work as part of a publishing venture. Infringement takes place when any one of the rights is violated: where, for example, a printer reproduces copies without selling them or a retailer sells copies without having anything to do with their reproduction. The references to "copies or phonorecords," although in the plural, are intended here and throughout the bill to include the singular (1 U.S.C. Sec. 1).

Reproduction.—Read together with the relevant definitions in section 101, the right "to reproduce the copyrighted work in copies or phonorecords" means the right to produce a material object in which the work is duplicated, transcribed, imitated, or simulated in a fixed form from which it can be "perceived, reproduced, or otherwise communicated, either directly or with the aid of a machine or device." As under the present law, a copyrighted work would be infringed by reproducing it in whole or in any substantial part, and by duplicating it exactly or by imitation or simulation. Wide departures or variations from the copyrighted work would still be an infringement as long as the author's "expression" rather than merely the author's "ideas" are taken. An exception to this general principle, applicable to the reproduction of copyrighted sound recordings, is specified in section 114.

"Reproduction" under clause (1) of section 106 is to be distinguished from "display" under clause (5). For a work to be "reproduced," its fixation in tangible form must be "sufficiently permanent or stable to permit it to be perceived, reproduced, or otherwise communicated for a period of more than transitory duration." Thus, the showing of images on a screen or tube would not be a violation of clause (1), although it might come within the scope of clause (5).

1. *Text of Section 107*

```
================================================================
```

   The following is a reprint of the entire text of section 107 of title
   17, United States Code.

```
================================================================
```

Section 107. Limitations on exclusive rights: Fair use

Notwithstanding the provisions of sections 106 and 106A, the fair use of a copyrighted work, including such use by reproduction in copies or phonorecords or by any other means specified by that section, for purposes such as criticism, comment, news reporting, teaching (including multiple copies for classroom use), scholarship, or research, is not an infringement of copyright. In determining whether the use made of a work in any particular case is a fair use the factors to be considered shall include—

(1) the purpose and character of the use, including whether such use is of a commercial nature or is for non-profit educational purposes;

(2) the nature of the copyrighted work;

(3) the amount and substantiality of the portion used in relation to the copyrighted work as a whole; and

(4) the effect of the use upon the potential market for or value of the copyrighted work.

The fact that a work is unpublished shall not itself bar a finding of fair use if such finding is made upon consideration of all the above factors.

2. Excerpts From House Report on Section 107

```
================================================================
```

   The following excerpts are reprinted from the House Report on the new
   copyright law (H.R. Rep. No. 94-1476, pages 65-74). The discussion
   of section 107 appears at pages 61-67 of the Senate Report (S. Rep.
   No. 94-473). The text of this section of the Senate Report is not
   reprinted in this booklet, but similarities and differences between
   the House and Senate Reports on particular points will be noted
   below.

```
================================================================
```

a. House Report: Introductory Discussion on Section 107

```
================================================================
```

The first two paragraphs in this portion of the House Report are closely similar to the Senate Report. The remainder of the passage differs substantially in the two Reports.**

```
================================================================
```

SECTION 107. FAIR USE
General background of the problem

The judicial doctrine of fair use, one of the most important and well-established limitations on the exclusive right of copyright owners, would be given express statutory recognition for the first time in section 107. The claim that a defendant's acts constituted a fair use rather than an infringement has been raised as a defense in innumerable copyright actions over the years, and there is ample case law recognizing the existence of the doctrine and applying it. The examples enumerated at page 24 of the Register's 1961 Report, while by no means exhaustive, give some idea of the sort of activities the courts might regard as fair use under the circumstances: "quotation of excerpts in a review or criticism for purposes of illustration or comment; quotation of short passages in a scholarly or technical work, for illustration or clarification of the author's observations; use in a parody of some of the content of the work parodied; summary of an address or article, with brief quotations, in a news report; reproduction by a library of a portion of a work to replace part of a damaged copy; reproduction by a teacher or student of a small part of a work to illustrate a lesson; reproduction of a work in legislative or judicial proceedings or reports; incidental and fortuitous reproduction, in a newsreel or broadcast, of a work located in the scene of an event being reported."

Although the courts have considered and ruled upon the fair use doctrine over and over again, no real definition of the concept has ever emerged. Indeed, since the doctrine is an equitable rule of reason, no generally applicable definition is possible, and each case raising the question must be decided on its own facts. On the other hand, the courts have evolved a set of criteria which, though in no case definitive or determinative, provide some gauge for balancing the equities. These criteria have been stated in various ways, but essentially they can all be reduced to the four standards which have been adopted in section 107: "(1) the purpose and character of the use, including whether such use is of a commercial nature or is for non-profit educational purposes; (2) the nature of the copyrighted work; (3) the amount and substantiality of the portion used in relation to the copyrighted work as a whole; and (4) the effect of the use upon the potential market for or value of the copyrighted work."

These criteria are relevant in determining whether the basic doctrine of fair use, as stated in the first sentence of section 107, applies in a particular case: "Notwithstanding the provisions of section 106, the fair use of a copyrighted work, including such use by reproduction in copies or phonorecords or by any other means specified by that section, for purposes such as criticism, comment, news reporting, teaching (including multiple copies for classroom use), scholarship, or research, is not an infringement of copyright."

The specific wording of section 107 as it now stands is the result of a process of accretion, resulting from the long controversy over the related problems of fair use and the reproduction (mostly by photocopying) of copyrighted material for educational and scholarly purposes. For example, the reference to fair use—"by reproduction in copies or phonorecords or by any other means"—is mainly intended to make clear that the doctrine has as much application to photocopying and taping as to older forms of use; it is not intended to give these kinds of reproduction any special status under the fair use provision or to sanction any reproduction beyond the normal and reasonable limits of fair use. Similarly, the newly-added reference to "multiple copies for classroom use" is a recognition that, under the proper circumstances of fairness, the doctrine can be applied to reproductions of multiple copies for the members of a class.

The Committee has amended the first of the criteria to be considered—"the purpose and character of the use"—to state explicitly that this factor includes a consideration of "whether such use is of a commercial nature or is for non-profit educational purposes." This amendment is not intended to be interpreted as any sort of not-for- profit limitation on educational uses of copyrighted works. It is an express recognition that, as under the present law, the commercial or non-profit character of an activity, while not conclusive with respect to fair use, can and should be weighed along with other factors in fair use decisions.

General intention behind the provision

The statement of the fair use doctrine in section 107 offers some guidance to users in determining when the principles of the doctrine apply. However, the endless variety of situations and combinations of circumstances that can rise in particular cases precludes the formulation of exact rules in the statute. The bill endorses the purpose and general scope of the judicial doctrine of fair use, but there is no disposition to freeze the doctrine in the statute, especially during a period of rapid technological change. Beyond a very broad statutory explanation of what fair use is and some of the criteria applicable to it, the courts must be free to adapt the doctrine to particular situations on a case-by-case basis. Section 107 is intended to restate the present judicial doctrine of fair use, not to change, narrow, or enlarge it in any way.

b. House Report: Statement of Intention as to Classroom Reproduction

===
The House Report differs substantially from the Senate Report on
this point.

===
(i) Introductory Statement

Intention as to classroom reproduction

Although the works and uses to which the doctrine of fair use is applicable are as broad as the copyright law itself, most of the discussion of section 107 has centered around questions of classroom reproduction, particularly photocopying. The arguments on the question are summarized at pp. 30-31 of this Committee's 1967 report (H.R. Rep. No. 83, 90th Cong., 1st Sess.), and have not changed materially in the intervening years.

The Committee also adheres to its earlier conclusion, that "a specific exemption freeing certain reproductions of copyrighted works for educational and scholarly purposes from copyright control is not justified." At the same time the Committee recognizes, as it did in 1967, that there is a "need for greater certainty and protection for teachers." In an effort to meet this need the Committee has not only adopted further amendments to section 107, but has also amended section 504(c) to provide innocent teachers and other non-profit users of copyrighted material with broad insulation against unwarranted liability for infringement. The latter amendments are discussed below in connection with Chapter 5 of the bill.

In 1967 the Committee also sought to approach this problem by including, in its report, a very thorough discussion of "the considerations lying behind the four criteria listed in the amended section 107, in the context of typical classroom situations arising today." This discussion appeared on pp. 32-35 of the 1967 report, and with some changes has been retained in the Senate report on S. 22 (S. Rep. No. 94-473, pp. 63-65). The Committee has reviewed this discussion, and considers that it still has value as an analysis of various aspects of the problem.

At the Judiciary Subcommittee hearings in June 1975, Chairman Kastenmeier and other members urged the parties to meet together independently in an effort to achieve a meeting of the minds as to permissible educational uses of copyrighted material. The response to these suggestions was positive, and a number of meetings of three groups, dealing respectively with classroon, reproduction of printed material, music, and audio-visual material, were held beginning in September 1975.

(ii) Guidelines With Respect to Books and Periodicals

In a joint letter to Chairman Kastenmeier, dated March 19, 1976, the representatives of the Ad Hoc Committee of Educational Institutions and Organizations on Copyright Law Revision, and of the Authors League of America, Inc., and the Association of American Publishers, Inc., stated:
"You may remember that in our letter of March 8, 1976 we told you that the negotiating teams representing authors and publishers and the Ad Hoc Group had reached tentative agreement on guidelines to insert in the Committee Report covering educational copying from books and periodicals under Section 107 of H.R. 2223 and S. 22, and that as part of that tentative agreement each side would accept the amendments to Sections 107 and 504 which were adopted by your Subcommittee on March 3,1976.

"We are now happy to tell you that the agreement has been approved by the principals and we enclose a copy herewith. We had originally intended to translate the agreement into language suitable for inclusion in the legislative report dealing with Section 107, but we have since been advised by committee staff that this will not be necessary.

"As stated above, the agreement refers only to copying from books and periodicals, and it is not intended to apply to musical or audiovisual works."

The full text of the agreement is as follows:

AGREEMENT ON GUIDELINES FOR CLASSROOM COPYING IN NOT-FOR-PROFIT EDUCATIONAL INSTITUTIONS WITH RESPECT TO BOOKS AND PERIODICALS
The purpose of the following guidelines is to state the minimum and not the maximum standards of educational fair use under Section 107 of H.R. 2223. The parties agree that the conditions determining the extent of permissible copying for educational purposes may change in the future; that certain types of copying permitted under these guidelines may not be permissible in the future; and conversely that in the future other types of copying not permitted under these guidelines may be permissible under revised guidelines.

Moreover, the following statement of guidelines is not intended to limit the types of copying permitted under the standards of fair use under judicial decision and which are stated in Section 107 of the Copyright Revision Bill. There may be instances in which copying which does not fall within the guidelines stated below may nonetheless be permitted under the criteria of fair use.

GUIDELINES
I. Single Copying for Teachers

A single copy may be made of any of the following by or for a teacher at his or her individual request for his or her scholarly research or use in teaching or preparation to teach a class:

A. A chapter from a book;

B. An article from a periodical or newspaper;

C. A short story, short essay or short poem, whether or not from a collective work;

D. A chart, graph, diagram, drawing, cartoon or picture from a book, periodical, or newspaper;

II. Multiple Copies for Classroom Use

Multiple copies (not to exceed in any event more than one copy per pupil in a course) may be made by or for the teacher giving the course for classroom use or discussion; provided that:

A. The copying meets the tests of brevity and spontaneity as defined below; and,

B. Meets the cumulative effect test as defined below; and,

C. Each copy includes a notice of copyright

Definitions

Brevity (i) Poetry: (a) A complete poem if less than 250 words and if printed on not more than two pages or, (b) from a longer poem, an excerpt of not more than 250 words.

(ii) Prose: (a) Either a complete article, story or essay of less than 2,500 words, or (b) an excerpt from any prose work of not more than 1,000 words or 10% of the work, whichever is less, but in any event a minimum of 500 words.

[Each of the numerical limits stated in "i" and "ii" above may be expanded to permit the completion of an unfinished line of a poem or of an unfinished prose paragraph.]

(iii) Illustration: One chart, graph, diagram, drawing, cartoon or picture per book or per periodical issue.

(iv) "Special" works: Certain works in poetry, prose or in "poetic prose" which often combine language with illustrations and which are intended sometimes for children and at other times for a more general audience fall short of 2,500 words in their entirety. Paragraph "ii" above notwithstandiiig such "special works" may not be reproduced in their entirety; however, an excerpt comprising not more than two of the published pages of such special work and containing not more than 10% of the words found in the text thereof, may be reproduced.

Spontaneity

(i) The copying is at the instance and inspiration of the individual teacher, and

(ii) The inspiration and decision to use the work and the moment of its use for maximum teaching effectiveness are so close in time that it would be unreasonable to expect a timely reply to a request for permission.

Cumulative Effect

(i) The copying of the material is for only one course in the school in which the copies are made.

(ii) Not more than one short poem, article, story, essay or two excerpts may be copied from the same author, nor more than three from the same collective work or periodical volume during one class term.

(iii) There shall not be more than nine instances of such multiple copying for one course during one class term.

[The limitations stated in "ii" and "iii" above shall not apply to current news periodicals and newspapers and current news sections of other periodicals.]

III. Prohibitions as to I and II Above

Notwithstanding any of the above, the following shall be prohibited:

(A) Copying shall not be used to create or to replace or substitute for anthologies, compilations or collective works. Such replacement or substitution may occur whether copies of various works or excerpts therefrom are accumulated or reproduced and used separately.

(B) There shall be no copying of or from works intended to be "consumable" in the course of study or of teaching. These include workbooks, exercises, standardized tests and test booklets and answer sheets and like consumable material.

(C) Copying shall not:

(a) substitute for the purchase of books, publishers' reprints or periodicals;

(b) be directed by higher authority;

(c) be repeated with respect to the same item by the same teacher from term to term.

(D) No charge shall be made to the student beyond the actual cost of the photocopying.

Agreed MARCH 19, 1976.

Ad Hoc Committee on Copyright Law Revision:
BY SHELDON ELLIOTT STEINBACH.
Author-Publisher Group:
Authors League of America:
BY IRWIN KARP, Counsel.
Association of American Publishers, Inc.:
BY ALEXANDER C. HOFFMAN, Chairman, Copyright Committee.
(iii) Guidelines With Respect to Music

In a joint letter dated April 30,1976, representatives of the Music Publishers' Association of the United States, Inc., the National Music Publishers' Association, Inc., the Music Teachers National Association, the Music Educators National Conference, the National Association of Schools of Music, and the Ad Hoc Committee on Copyright Law Revision, wrote to Chairman Kastenmeier as follows:

"During the hearings on H.R. 2223 in June 1975, you and several of your subcommittee members suggested that concerned groups should work together in developing guidelines which would be helpful to clarify Section 107 of the bill.

"Representatives of music educators and music publishers delayed their meetings until guidelines had been developed relative to books and periodicals. Shortly after that work was completed and those guidelines were forwarded to your subcommittee, representatives of the undersigned music organizations met together with representatives of the Ad Hoc Committee on Copyright Law Revision to draft guidelines relative to music.

"We are very pleased to inform you that the discussions thus have been fruitful on the guidelines which have been developed. Since private music teachers are an important factor in music education, due consideration has been given to the concerns of that group.

"We trust that this will be helpful in the report on the bill to clarify
Fair Use as it applies to music."
The text of the guidelines accompanying this letter is as follows:

GUIDELINES FOR EDUCATIONAL USES OF MUSIC
The purpose of the following guidelines is to state the minimum and not the maximum standards of educational fair use under Section 107 of HR 2223. The parties agree that the conditions determining the extent of permissible copying for educational purposes may change in the future; that certain types of copying permitted under these guidelines may not be permissible in the future, and conversely that in the future other types of copying not permitted under these guidelines may be permissible under revised guidelines.

Moreover, the following statement of guidelines is not intended to limit the types of copying permitted under the standards of fair use under judicial decision and which are stated in Section 107 of the Copyright Revision Bill. There may be instances in which copying which does not fall within the guidelines stated below may nonetheless be permitted under the criteria of fair use.

A. Permissible Uses

1. Emergency copying to replace purchased copies which for any reason are not available for an imminent performance provided purchased replacement copies shall be substituted in due course.

2. For academic purposes other than performance, single or multiple copies of excerpts of works may be made, provided that the excerpts do not comprise a part of the whole which would constitute a performable unit such as a section [1], movement or aria, but in no case more than 10 percent of the whole work. The number of copies shall not exceed one copy per pupil. [2]

3. Printed copies which have been purchased may be edited or simplified provided that the fundamental character of the work is not distorted or the lyrics, if any, altered or lyrics added if none exist.

4. A single copy of recordings of performances by students may be made for evaluation or rehearsal purposes and may be retained by the educational institution or individual teacher.

5. A single copy of a sound recording (such as a tape, disc or cassette) of copyrighted music may be made from sound recordings owned by an educational institution or an individual teacher for the purpose of constructing aural exercises or examinations and may be retained by the educational institution or individual teacher. (This pertains only to the copyright of the music itself and not to any copyright which may exist in the sound recording.)

B. Prohibitions

1. Copying to create or replace or substitute for anthologies, compilations or collective works.

2. Copying of or from works intended to be "consumable" in the course of study or of teaching such as workbooks, exercises, standardized tests and answer sheets and like material.

3. Copying for the purpose of performance, except as in A(1) above.

4. Copying for the purpose of substituting for the purchase of music, except as in A(1) and A(2) above.

5. Copying without inclusion of the copyright notice which appears on the printed copy.

(iv) Discussion of Guidelines

The Committee appreciates and commends the efforts and the cooperative ancl reasonable spirit of the parties who achieved the agreed guidelines on books and periodicals and on music. Representatives of the American Association of University Professors and of the Association of American Law Schools have written to the Committee strongly criticizing the guidelines, particularly with respect to multiple copying, as being too restrictive with respect to classroom situations at the university and graduate level. However, the Committee notes that the Ad Hoc group did include representatives of higher education, that the stated "purpose of the . . . guidelines is to state the minimum and not the maximum standards of educational fair use" and that the agreement acknowledges "there may be instances in which copying which does not fall within the guidelines . . . may nonetheless be permitted under the criteria of fair use."

The Committee believes the guidelines are a reasonable interpretation of the minimum standards of fair use. Teachers will know that copying within the guidelines is fair use. Thus, the guidelines serve the purpose of fulfilling the need for greater certainty and protection for teachers. The Committee expresses the hope that if there are areas where standards other than these guidelines may be appropriate, the parties will continue their efforts to provide additional specific guidelines in the same spirit of good will and give and take that has marked the discussion of this subject in recent months.

c. House Report: Additional Excerpts

The concentrated attention given the fair use provision in the context of classroom teaching
activities should not obscure its application in other areas. It must be emphasized again that
the same general standards of fair use are applicable to all kinds of uses of copyrighted
material, although the relative weight to be given them will differ from case to case.

* * *

A problem of particular urgency is that of preserving for posterity prints of motion pictures
made before 1942. Aside from the deplorable fact that in a great many cases the only existing
copy of a film has been deliberately destroyed, those that remain are in immediate danger of
disintegration; they were printed on film stock with a nitrate base that will inevitably
decompose in time. The efforts of the Library of Congress, the American Film Institute, and
other organizations to rescue and preserve this irreplaceable contribution to our cultural life
are to be applauded, and the making of duplicate copies for purposes of archival preservation
certanly falls within the scope of "fair use."

* * *

During the consideration of the revision bill in the 94th Congress it was proposed that
independent newsletters, as distinguished from house organs and publicity or advertising
publications, be given separate treatment. It is argued that newsletters are particularly
vulnerable to mass photocopying, and that most newsletters have fairly modest circulations.
Whether the copying of portions of a newsletter is an act of infringement or a fair use will
necessarily turn on the facts of the individual case. However, as a general principle, it seems
clear that the scope of the fair use doctrine should be considerably narrower in the case of
newsletters than in that of either mass-circulation periodicals or scientific journals. The
commercial nature of the user is a significant factor in such cases: Copying by a profit-making
user of even a small portion of a newsletter may have a significant impact on the commercial
market for the work.

The Committee has examined the use of excerpts from copyrighted works in the art work of
calligraphers. The committee believes that a single copy reproduction of an excerpt from a
copyrighted work by a calligrapher for a single client does not represent an infringement of
copyright. Likewise, a single reproduction of excerpts from a copyrighted work by a student
calligrapher or teacher in a learning situation would be a fair use of the copyrighted work.

The Register of Copyrights has recommended that the committee report describe the
relationship between this section and the provisions of section 108 relating to reproduction
by libraries and archives. The doctrine of fair use applies to library photocopying, and nothing
contained in section 108 "in any way affects the right of fair use." No provision of section
108 is intended to take away any rights existing under the fair use doctrine. To the contrary,
section 108 authorizes certain photocopying practices which may not qualify as a fair use.

The criteria of fair use are necessarily set forth in general terms. In the application of the
criteria of fair use to specific photocopying practices of libraries, it is the intent of this

legislation to provide an appropriate balancing of the rights of creators, and the needs of users.

3. Excerpts From Conference Report on Section 107

==
The following excerpt is reprinted from the Report of the
Conference Committee on the new copyright law (H.R. Rep. No. 94-1733,
page 70).

==
FAIR USE
Senate bill

The Senate bill, in section 107, embodied express statutory recognition of the judicial doctrine that the fair use of a copyrighted work is not an infringement of copyright. It set forth the fair use doctrine, including four criteria for determining its applicability in particular cases, in general terms.

House bill

The House bill amended section 107 in two respects: in the general statement of the fair use doctrine it added a specific reference to multiple copies for classroom use, and it amplified the statement of the first of the criteria to be used in judging fair use (the purpose and character of the use) by referring to the commercial nature or nonprofit educational purpose of the use.

Conference substitute

The conference substitute adopts the House amendments. The conferees accept as part of their understanding of fair use the Guidelines for Classroom Copying in Not-for-Profit Educational Institutions with respect to books and periodicals appearing at pp. 68-70 of the House Report (H. Rept. No. 94-1476, as corrected at p. H 10727 of the Congressional Record for September 21, 1976), and for educational uses of music appearing at pp. 70-71 of the House report, as amended in the statement appearing at p. H 10875 of the Congressional Record of September 22, 1976. The conferees also endorse the statement concerning the meaning of the word "teacher" in the guidelines for books and periodicals, and the application of fair use in the case of use of television programs within the confines of a nonprofit educational institution for the deaf and hearing impaired, both of which appear on p. H 10875 of the Congressional Record of September 22, 1976.

4. Excerpts From Congressional Debates

==
The following excerpts are reprinted from the Congressional Record of September 22, 1976, including statements by Mr. Kastenmeier (Chairman of the House Judiciary Subcommittee responsible for the bill) on the floor of the House of Representatives.
==

MR. KASTENMEIER.

* * *

Mr. Chairman, before concluding my remarks I would like to discuss several questions which have been raised concerning the meaning of several provisions of S. 22 as reported by the House Judiciary Committee and of statements in the committee's report, No. 94-1476.

* * *

Another question involves the reference to "teacher" in the "Agreement on Guidelines for Classroom Copying in Not-for-Profit Educational Institutions" reproduced at pages 68-70 of the committee's report No. 94-1476 in connection with section 107. It has been pointed out that, in planning his or her teaching on a day-to-day basis in a variety of educational situations, an individual teacher will commonly consult with instructional specialists on the staff of the school, such as reading specialists, curriculum specialists, audiovisual directors, guidance counselors, and the like. As long as the copying meets all of the other criteria laid out in the guidelines, including the requirements for spontaneity and the prohibition against the copying being directed by higher authority, the committee regards the concept of "teacher" as broad enough to include instructional specialists working in consultation with actual instructors.

Also in consultation with section 107, the committee's attention has been directed to the unique educational needs and problems of the approximately 50,000 deaf and hearing-impaired students in the United States, and the inadequacy of both public and commercial television to serve their educational needs. It has been suggested that, as long as clear-cut constraints are imposed and enforced, the doctrine of fair use is broad enough to permit the making of an off-the-air fixation of a television program within a non-profit educational institution for the deaf and hearing impaired, the reproduction of a master and a work copy of a captioned version of the original fixation, and the performance of the program from the work copy within the confines of the institution. In identifying the constraints that would have to be imposed within an institution in order for these activities to be considered as fair use, it has been suggested that the purpose of the use would have to be non-commercial in every respect, and educational in the sense that it serves as part of a deaf or hearing-impaired student's learning environment within the institution, and that the institution would have to insure that the master and work copy would remain in the hands of a limited number of authorized personnel within the institution, would be responsible for assuring against its unauthorized reproduction or distribution, or its performance or retention for other than educational purposes within the institution. Work copies of captioned programs could be shared among institutions for the deaf abiding by the constraints specified. Assuming that these constraints are both imposed and enforced, and that no other factors intervene to render the use unfair, the committee believes that the activities described could reasonably be considered fair use under section 107.

* * *

Mr. Chairman, because of the complexity of this bill and the delicate balances which it creates among competing economic interests, the committee will resist extensive amendment of this bill. On behalf of the committee I would urge all of my colleagues to vote favorably on Sec. 22.

Mr. SKUBITZ. Mr. Chairman, will the gentleman yield?

Mr. KASTENMEIER. I am happy to yield to my friend, the gentleman from Kansas.

Mr. SKUBITZ. Mr. Chairman, I thank my friend, the gentleman from Wisconsin, for yielding.

Mr. Chairman, I have received a great deal of mail from the schoolteachers in my district who are particularly concerned about section 107—fair use—the fair use of copyrighted material. Having been a former schoolteacher myself, I believe they make a good point and there is a sincere fear on their part that, because of the vagueness or ambiguity in the bill's treatment of the doctrine of fair use, they may subject themselves to liability for an unintentional infringement of copyright when all they were trying to do was the job for which they were trained.

The vast majority of teachers in this country would not knowingly infringe upon a person's copyright, but, as any teacher can appreciate, there are times when information is needed and is available, but it may be literally impossible to locate the right person to approve the use of that material and the purchase of such would not be feasible and, in the meantime, the teacher may have lost that "teachable moment."

Did the subcommittee take these problems into consideration and did they do anything to try and help the teachers to better understand section 107?

Have the teachers been protected by this section 107?

Mr. KASTENMEIER. Mr. Chairman, in response to the gentleman's question and his observations preceding the question, I would say, indeed they have.

Over the years this has been one of the most difficult questions. It is a problem that I believe has been very successfully resolved.

Section 107 on "Fair Use" has, of course, restated four standards, and these standards are, namely: The purpose and character of the use of the material; the nature of the copyrighted work; the amount and substantiality of the portion used in relation to the copyrighted work as a whole; and the effect of the use upon the potential market for or value of the copyrighted work.

These are the four "Fair Use" criteria. These alone were not adequate to guide teachers, and I am sure the gentleman from Kansas (Mr. SKUBITZ) understands that as a schoolteacher himself.

Therefore, the educators, the proprietors, and the publishers of educational materials did, at the committee's long insistence, get together. While there were many fruitless meetings, they did finally get together.

Mr. Chairman, I will draw the gentleman's attention to pages 65 through 74 in the report which contain extensive guidelines for teachers. I am very happy to say that there was an agreement reached between teachers and publishers of educational material, and that today the National Education Association supports the bill, and it has, in fact, sent a telegram which at the appropriate time I will make a part of the RECORD and which requests support for the bill in its present form, believing that it has satisfied the needs of the teachers:

***

NATIONAL EDUCATION ASSOCIATION,
Washington, D.C., September 10, 1976.
National Education Association urgently requests your support of the Copyright Revision bill, H.R. 2223, as reported by the Judiciary Committee. This compromise effort represents a

major breakthrough in establishing equitable legal guidelines for the use of copyright materials for instructional and research purposes. We ask your support of the committee bill without amendments.

JAMES W. GREEN, Assistant Director for Legislation. ***

Mr. SKUBITZ. Mr. Chairman, if the gentleman will yield further, then the NEA is satisfied with the language in the bill as it now stands; is that correct?

Mr. KASTENMEIER. The gentleman is correct.

Mr. SKUBITZ. Mr. Chairman, I thank the gentleman.

——————————————————————————— D.　REPRODUCTION　BY LIBRARIES AND ARCHIVES ———————————————————————————

1. Text of Section 108

==
The following is a reprint of the entire text of section 108 of title 17, United States Code.
==

Section 108. Limitations on exclusive rights:
Reproduction by libraries and archives

(a) Notwithstanding the provisions of section 106, it is not an infringement of copyright for a library or archives, or any of its employees acting within the scope of their employment, to reproduce no more than one copy or phonorecord of a work, or to distribute such copy or phonorecord, under the conditions specified by this section, if—

(1) the reproduction or distribution is made without any purpose of direct or indirect commercial advantage;

(2) the collections of the library or archives are (i) open to the public, or (ii) available not only to researchers affiliated with the library or archives or with the institution of which it is a part, but also to other persons doing research in a specialized field; and

(3) the reproduction or distribution of the work includes a notice of copyright.

(b) The rights of reproduction and distribution under this section apply to a copy or phonorecord of an unpublished work duplicated in facsimile form solely for purposes of preservation and security or for deposit for research use in another library or archives of the type described by clause (2) of subsection (a), if the copy or phonorecord reproduced is currently in the collections of the library or archives.

(c) The right of reproduction under this section applies to a copy or phonorecord of a published work duplicated in facsimile form solely for the purpose of replacement of a copy or phonorecord that is damaged, deteriorating, lost, or stolen, if the library or archives has, after a reasonable effort, determined that an unused replacement cannot be obtained at a fair price.

(d) The rights of reproduction and distribution under this section apply to a copy, made from the collection of a library or archives where the user makes his or her request or from that of another library or archives, of no more than one article or other contribution to a copyrighted collection or periodical issue, or to a copy or phonorecord of a small part of any other copyrighted work, if—

(1) the copy or phonorecord becomes the property of the user, and the library or archives has had no notice that the copy or phonorecord would be used for any purpose other than private study, scholarship, or research; and

(2) the library or archives displays prominently, at the place where orders are accepted, and includes on its order form, a warning of copyright in accordance with requirements that the Register of Copyrights shall prescribe by regulation.

(e) The rights of reproduction and distribution under this section apply to the entire work, or to a substantial part of it, made from the collection of a library or archives where the user makes his or her request or from that of another library or archives, if the library or archives. has first determined, on the basis of a reasonable investigation, that a copy or phonorecord of the copyrighted work cannot be obtained at a fair price, if—

(1) the copy or phonorecord becomes the property of the user, and the library or archives has had no notice that the copy or phonorecord would be used for any purpose other than private study, scholarship, or research; and

(2) the library or archives displays prominently, at the place where orders are accepted, and includes on its order form, a warning of copyright in accordance with requirements that the Register of Copyrights shall prescribe by regulation.

(f) Nothing in this section—

(1) shall be construed to impose liability for copyright infringement upon a library or archives or its employees for the unsupervised use of reproducing equipment located on its premises: Provided, That such equipment displays a notice that the making of a copy may be subject to the copyright law;

(2) excuses a person who uses such reproducing equipment or who requests a copy or phonorecord under subsection (d) from liability for copyright infringement for any such act, or for any later use of such copy or phonorecord, if it exceeds fair use as provided by section 107;

(3) shall be construed to limit the reproduction and distribution by lending of a limited number of copies and excerpts by a library or archives of an audiovisual news program, subject to clauses (1), (2), and (3) of subsection (a); or

(4) in any way affects the right of fair use as provided by section 107, or any contractual obligations assumed at any time by the library or archives when it obtained a copy or phonorecord of a work in its collections.

(g) The rights of reproduction and distribution under this section extend to the isolated and unrelated reproduction or distribution of a single copy or phonorecord of the same material on separate occasions, but do not extend to cases where the library or archives, or its employee—

(1) is aware or has substaiitial reason to believe that it is engaging in the related or concerted reproduction or distribution of multiple copies or phonorecords of the same material, whether made on one occasion or over a period of time, and whether intended for aggregate use by one or more individuals or for separate use by the individual members of a group; or

(2) engages in the systematic reproduction or distribution of single or multiple copies or phonorecords of material described in subsection (d): Provided, That nothing in this clause prevents a library or archives from participating in interlibrary arrangements that do not have, as their purpose or effect, that the library or archives receiving such copies or phonorecords for distribution does so in such aggregate quantities as to substitute for a subscription to or purchase of such work.

(h) The rights of reproduction and distribution under this section do not apply to a musical work, a pictorial, graphic or sculptural work, or a motion picture or other audiovisual work other than an audiovisual work dealing with news, except that no such limitation shall apply with respect to rights granted by subsections (b) and (c), or with respect to pictorial or graphic works published as illustrations, diagrams, or similar adjuncts to works of which copies are reproduced or distributed in accordance with subsections (d) and (e).

2. Excerpts From Senate Report on Section 108

===
The following excerpts are reprinted from the 1975 Senate Report on the new copyright law (S. Rep. No. 94-473, pages 67-71). Where the discussions of particular points are generally similar in the two Reports, the passages from the later House Report are reprinted in this booklet. Where the discussion of particular points is substantially different, passages from both   Reports   are   reprinted.
===

a. Senate Report: Discussion of Libraries and Archives in Profit-Making Institutions

The limitation of section 108 to reproduction and distribution by libraries and archives "without any purpose of direct or indirect commercial advantage" is intended to preclude a library or archives in a profit-making organization from providing photocopies of copyrighted materials to employees engaged in furtherance of the organization's commercial enterprise, unless such copying qualifies as a fair use, or the organization has obtained the necessary copyright licenses. A commercial organization should purchase the number of copies of a work that it requires, or obtain the consent of the copyright owner to the making of the photocopies.

b. Senate Report: Discussion of Multiple Copies and Systematic Reproduction

Multiple copies and systematic reproduction

Subsection (g) provides that the rights granted by this section extend only to the "isolated and unrelated reproduction of a single copy," but this section does not authorize the related or concerted reproduction of multiple copies of the same material whether made on one occasion or over a period of time, and whether intended for aggregate use by one individual or for separate use by the individual members of a group. For example, if a college professor instructs his class to read an article from a copyrighted journal, the school library would not be permitted, under subsection (g), to reproduce copies of the article for the members of the class.

Subsection (g) also provides that section 108 does not authorize the systematic reproduction or distribution of copies or phonorecords of articles or other contributions to copyrighted collections or periodicals or of small parts of other copyrighted works whether or not multiple copies are reproduced or distributed. Systematic reproduction or distribution occurs when a library makes copies of such materials available to other libraries or to groups of users under formal or informal arrangements whose purpose or effect is to have the reproducing library serve as their source of such material. Such systematic reproduction and distribution, as distinguished from isolated and unrelated reproduction or distribution, may substitute the copies reproduced by the source library for subscriptions or reprints or other copies which the receiving libraries or users might otherwise have purchased for themselves, from the publisher or the licensed reproducing agencies.

While it is not possible to formulate specific definitions of "systematic copying," the following examples serve to illustrate some of the copying prohibited by subsection (g).

(1) A library with a collection of journals in biology informs other libraries with similar collections that it will maintain and build its own collection and will make copies of articles from these journals available to them and their patrons on request. Accordingly, the other libraries discontinue or refrain from purchasing subscriptions to these journals and fulfill their patrons' requests for articles by obtaining photocopies from the source library.

(2) A research center employing a number of scientists and technicians subscribes to one or two copies of needed periodicals. By reproducing photocopies of articles the center is able to make the material in these periodicals available to its staff in the same manner which otherwise would have required multiple subscriptions.

(3) Several branches of a library system agree that one branch will subscribe to particular journals in lieu of each branch purchasing its own subscriptions, and the one subscribing branch will reproduce copies of articles from the publication for users of the other branches.

The committee believes that section 108 provides an appropriate statutory balancing of the rights of creators and the needs of users. However, neither a statute nor legislative history can specify precisely which library photocopying practices constitute the making of "single copies" as distinguished from "systematic reproduction." Isolated single spontaneous requests must be distinguished from "systematic reproduction." The photocopying needs of such operations as multi-county regional systems must be met. The committee therefore recommends that representatives of authors, book and periodical publishers and other owners of copyrighted material meet with the library community to formulate photocopying guidelines to assist library patrons and employees. Concerning library photocopying practices not authorized by this legislation, the committee recommends that workable clearance and licensing procedures be developed.

It is still uncertain how far a library may go under the Copyright Act of 1909 in supplying a photocopy of copyrighted material in its collection. The recent case of The Williams and Wilkins Company v. The United States failed to significantly illuminate the application of the fair use doctrine to library photocopying practices. Indeed, the opinion of the Court of Claims said the Court was engaged in "a 'holding Operation' in the interim period before Congress enacted its preferred solution."

While the several opinions in the Wilkins case have given the Congress little guidance as to the current state of the law on fair use, these opinions provide additional support for the balanced resolution of the photocopying issue adopted by the Senate last year in S. 1361 and preserved in section 108 of this legislation. As the Court of Claims opinion succinctly stated "there is much to be said on all sides."

In adopting these provisions on library photocopying, the committee is aware that through such programs as those of the National Commission on Libraries and Information Science there will be a significant evolution in the functioning and services of libraries. To consider the possible need for changes in copyright law and procedures as a result of new technology, a National Commission on New Technological Uses of Copyrighted Works has been established (Public Law 93-573).

3. Excerpts From House Report on Section 108

==
The following excerpts are reprinted from the House Report on the new copyright law (H.R. Rep. No. 94-1476, pages 74-79). All of the House Report's discussion of section 108 is reprinted here; similarities and differences between the House and Senate Reports on particular points will be noted below.
==

a. House Report: Introductory Statement

==
   This paragraph is substantially the same in the Senate and House
   Reports.

==
Notwithstanding the exclusive rights of the owners of copyright, section 108 provides that under certain conditions it is not an infringement of copyright for a library or archives, or any of its employees acting within the scope of their employment, to reproduce or distribute not more than one copy or phonorecord of a work, provided (1) the reproduction or distribution is made without any purpose of direct or indirect commercial advantage and (2) the collections of the library or archives are open to the public or available not only to researchers affiliated with the library or archives, but also to other persons doing research in a specialized field, and (3) the reproduction or distribution of the work includes a notice of copyright.

b. House Report: Discussion of Libraries and Archives in Profit-Making Institutions

==
The Senate and House Reports differ substantially on this point. The Senate Report's discussion is reprinted at page 17, above.
==

Under this provision, a purely commercial enterprise could not establish a collection of copyrighted works, call itself a library or archive, and engage in for-profit reproduction and distribution of photocopies. Similarly, it would not be possible for a non-profit institution, by means of contractual arrangements with a commercial copying enterprise, to authorize the enterprise to carry out copying and distribution functions that would be exempt if conducted by the non-profit institution itself.

The reference to "indirect commercial advantage" has raised questions as to the status of photocopying done by or for libraries or archival collections within industrial, profitmaking, or proprietary institutions (such as the research and development departments of chemical, pharmaceutical, automobile, and oil corporations, the library of a propriatary hospital, the collections owned by a law or medical partnership, etc.).

There is a direct interrelationship between this problem and the prohibitions against "multiple" and "systematic" photocopying in section 108 (g) (1) and (2). Under section 108, a library in a profit-making organization would not be authorized to:

(a) use a single subscription or copy to supply its employees with multiple copies of material relevant to their work; or

(b) use a single subscription or copy to supply its employees, on request, with single copies of material relevant to their work, where the arrangement is "systematic" in the sense of deliberately substituting photocopying for subscription or purchase; or

(c) use "interlibrary loan" arrangements for obtaining photocopies in such aggregate quantities as to substitute for subscriptions or purchase of material needed by employees in their work.

Moreover, a library in a profit-making organization could not evade these obligations by installing reproducing equipment on its premises for unsupervised use by the organization's staff.

Isolated, spontaneous making of single photocopies by a library in a for-profit organization, without any systematic effort to substitute photocopying for subscriptions or purchases, would be covered by section 108, even though the copies are furnished to the employees of the organization for use in their work. Similarly, for-profit libraries could participate in interlibrary arrangements for exchange of photocopies, as long as the reproduction or distribution was not "systematic." These activities, by themselves, would ordinarily not be considered "for direct or indirect commercial advantage," since the "advantage" referred to in this clause must attach to the immediate commercial motivation behind the reproduction or distribution itself, rather than to the ultimate profit-making motivation behind the enterprise in which the library is located. On the other hand, section 108 would not excuse reproduction or distribution if there were a commercial motive behind the actual making or distributing of the copies, if multiple copies were made or distributed, or if the photocopying activities were "systematic" in the sense that their aim was to substitute for subscriptions or purchases.

c. House Report: Rights of Reproduction and Distribution Under
   Section 108

==
   The following paragraphs are closely similar in the Senate and House
   Reports.

==
The rights of reproduction and distribution under section 108 apply in the following circumstances:

Archival reproductions

Subsection (b) authorizes the reproduction and distribution of a copy or phonorecord of an unpublished work duplicated in facsimile form solely for purposes of preservation and security, or for deposit for research use in another library or archives, if the copy or phonorecord reproduced is currently in the collections of the first library or archives. Only unpublished works could be reproduced under this exemption, but the right would extend to any type of work, including photographs, motion pictures and sound recordings.

Under this exemption, for example, a repository could make photocopies of manuscripts by microfilm or electrostatic process, but could not reproduce the work in "machine-readable" language for storage in an information system.

Replacement of damaged copy

Subsection (c) authorizes the reproduction of a published work duplicated in facsimile form solely for the purpose of replacement of a copy or phonorecord that is damaged, deteriorating, lost or stolen, if the library or archives has, after a reasonable effort, determined that an unused replacement cannot be obtained at a fair price. The scope and nature of a reasonable investigation to determine that an unused replacement cannot be obtained will vary according to the circumstances of a particular situation. It will always require recourse to commonly-known trade sources in the United States, and in the normal situation also to the publisher or other copyright owner (if such owner can be located at the address listed in the copyright registration), or an authorized reproducing service.

Articles and small excerpts

Subsection (d) authorizes the reproduction and distribution of a copy of not more than one article or other contribution to a copyrighted collection or periodical issue, or of a copy or phonorecord of a small part of any other copyrighted work. The copy or phonorecord may be made by the library where the user makes his request or by another library pursuant to an interlibrary loan. It is further required that the copy become the property of the user, that the library or archives have no notice that the copy would be used for any purposes other than private study, scholarship or research, and that the library or archives display prominently at the place where reproduction requests are accepted, and includes in its order form, a warning of copyright in accordance with requirements that the Register of Copyrights shall prescribe by regulation.

Out-of-print works

Subsection (e) authorizes the reproduction and distribution of a copy or phonorecord of an entire work under certain circumstances, if it has been established that a copy cannot be obtained at a fair price. The copy may be made by the library where the user makes his request or by another library pursuant to an interlibrary loan. The scope and nature of a reasonable investigation to determine that an unused copy cannot be obtained will vary according to the circumstances of a particular situation. It will always require recourse to commonly-known trade sources in the United States, and in the normal situation also to the publisher or other copyright owner (if the owner can be located at the address listed in the copyright registration), or an authorized reproducing service. It is further required that the copy become the property of the user, that the library or archives have no notice that the copy would be used for any purpose other than private study, scholarship, or research, and that the library or archives display prominently at the place where reproduction requests are accepted, and include on its order form, a warning of copyright in accordance with requirements that the Register of Copyrights shall prescribe by regulation.

d. House Report: General Exemptions for Libraries and Archives

==
    Parts of the following paragraphs are substantially similar in the
    Senate and House Reports. Differences in the House Report on certain
    points reflect certain amendments in section 108(f) and elsewhere
    in the Copyright Act.

==
General exemptions

Clause (1) of subsection (f) specifically exempts a library or archives or its employees from liability for the unsupervised use of reproducing equipment located on its premises, provided that the reproducing equipment displays a notice that the making of a copy may be subject to the copyright law. Clause (2) of subsection (f) makes clear that this exemption of the library or archives does not extend to the person using such equipment or requesting such copy if the use exceeds fair use. Insofar as such person is concerned the copy or phonorecord made is not considered "lawfully" made for purposes of sections 109, 110 or other provisions of the title.

Clause (3) provides that nothing in section 108 is intended to limit the reproduction and distribution by lending of a limited number of copies and excerpts of an audio-visual news program. This exemption is intended to apply to the daily newscasts of the national television networks, which report the major events of the day. It does not apply to documentary (except documentary programs involving news reporting as that term is used in section 107), magazine-format or other public affairs broadcasts dealing with subjects of general interest to the viewing public.

The clause was first added to the revision bill in 1974 by the adoption of an amendment proposed by Senator Baker. It is intended to permit libraries and archives, subject to the general conditions of this section, to make off-the-air videotape recordings of daily network newscasts for limited distribution to scholars and researchers for use in research purposes. As such, it is an adjunct to the American Television and Radio Archive established in Section 113 of the Act which will be the principal repository for television broadcast material, including news broadcasts. The inclusion of language indicating that such material may only be distributed by lending by the library or archive is intended to preclude performance, copying, or sale, whether or not for profit, by the recipient of a copy of a television broadcast taped off-the-air pursuant to this clause.

Clause (4), in addition to asserting that nothing contained in section 108 "affects the right of fair use as provided by section 107," also provides that the right of reproduction granted by this section does not override any contractual arrangements assumed by a library or archives when it obtained a work for its collections. For example, if there is an express contractual prohibition against reproduction for any purpose, this legislation shall not be construed as justifying a violation of the contract. This clause is intended to encompass the situation where an individual makes papers, manuscripts or other works available to a library with the understanding that they will not be reproduced.

It is the intent of this legislation that a subsequent unlawful use by a user of a copy or phonorecord of a work lawfully made by a library, shall not make the library liable for such improper use.

e. House Report: Discussion of Multiple Copies and Systematic Reproduction

==
The Senate and House Reports differ substantially on this point. The Senate Report's discussion is reprinted at page 17. above.
==

Multiple copies and systematic reproduction

Subsection (g) provides that the rights granted by this section extend only to the "isolated and unrelated reproduction of a single copy or phonorecord of the same material on separate occasions." However, this section does not authorize the related or concerted reproduction of multiple copies or phonorecords of the same material, whether made on one occasion or over a period of time, and whether intended for aggregate use by one individual or for separate use by the individual members of a group.

With respect to material described in subsection (d)—articles or other contributions to periodicals or collections, and small parts of other copyrighted works—subsection (g) (2) provides that the exemptions of section 108 do not apply if the library or archive engages in "systematic reproduction or distribution of single or multiple copies or phonorecords." This provision in S.22 provoked a storm of controversy, centering around the extent to which the restrictions on "systematic" activities would prevent the continuation and development of interlibrary networks and other arrangements involving the exchange of photocopies. After thorough consideration, the Committee amended section 108 (g) (2) to add the following proviso:

Provided, that nothing in this clause prevents a library or archives from participating in interlibrary arrangements that do not have, as their purpose or effect, that the library or archives receiving such copies or phonorecords for distribution does so in such aggregate quantities as to substitute for a subscription to or purchase of such work.

In addition, the Committee added a new subsection (i) to section 108, requiring the Register of Copyrights, five years from the effective date of the new Act and at five year intervals thereafter, to report to Congress upon "the extent to which this section has achieved the intended statutory balancing of the rights of creators, and the needs of users," and to make appropriate legislative or other recommendations. As noted in connection with section 107, the Committee also amended section 504(c) in a way that would insulate librarians from unwarranted liability for copyright infringement; this amendment is discussed below.

The key phrases in the Committee's amendment of section 108(g) (2) are "aggregate quantities" and "substitute for a subscription to or purchase of" a work. To be implemented effectively in practice, these provisions will require the development and implementation of more-or-less specific guidelines establishing criteria to govern various situations. The National Commission on New Technological Uses of Copyrighted Works (CONTU) offered to provide good offices in helping to develop these guidelines. This offer was accepted and, although the final text of guidelines has not yet been achieved, the Committee has reason to hope that, within the next month, some agreement can be reached on an initial set of guidelines covering practices under section 108(g)(2).

f. House Report: Discussion of Works Excluded

===
The House Report's discussion of section 108(h) is longer than the corresponding paragraph
in   the   Senate   Report,   and   reflects   certain   amendments   in   the   subsection.
===

Works excluded

Subsection (h) provides that the rights of reproduction and distribution under this section do
not apply to a musical work, a pictorial, graphic or sculptural work, or a motion picture or
other audiovisual work other than "an audiovisual work dealing with news." The latter term
is intended as the equivalent in meaning of the phrase "audio-visual news program" in section
108 (f) (3). The exclusions under subsection (h) do not apply to archival reproduction under
subsection (b), to replacement of damaged or lost copies or phonorecords under subsection
(c), or to "pictorial or graphic works published as illustrations, diagrams, or similar adjuncts
to works of which copies are reproduced or distributed in accordance with subsections (d)
and (e)."

Although subsection (h) generally removes musical, graphic, and audiovisual works from the
specific exemptions of section 108, it is important to recognize that the doctrine of fair use
under section 107 remains fully applicable to the photocopying or other reproduction of such
works. In the case of music, for example, it would be fair use for a scholar doing musicological
research to have a library supply a copy of a portion of a score or to reproduce portions of a
phonorecord of a work. Nothing in section 108 impairs the applicability of the fair use
doctrine to a wide variety of situations involving photocopying or other reproduction by a
library of copyrighted material in its collections, where the user requests the reproduction for
legitimate scholarly or research purposes.

4. Excerpts From Conference Report

===
   The following excerpt is reprinted from the Report of the Conference
   Committee on the new copyright law (H.R. Rep. No. 94-1733, pages
   70-74).

===
a. Conference Report: Introductory Discussion of Section 108

REPRODUCTION BY LIBRARIES AND ARCHIVES
Senate bill

Section 108 of the Senate bill dealt with a variety of situations involving photocopying and
other forms of reproduction by libraries and archives. It specified the conditions under which
single copies of copyrighted material can be noncommercially reproduced and distributed,
but made clear that the privileges of a library or archives under the section do not apply where
the reproduction or distribution is of multiple copies or is "systematic." Under subsection (f),
the section was not to be construed as limiting the reproduction and distribution, by a library
or archive meeting the basic criteria of the section, of a limited number of copies and excerpts
of an audiovisual news program.

House bill

The House bill amended section 108 to make clear that, in cases involving interlibrary arrangements for the exchange of photocopies, the activity would not be considered "systematic" as long as the library or archives receiving the reproductions for distribution does not do so in such aggregate quantities as to substitute for a subscription to or purchase of the work. A new subsection (i) directed the Register of Copyrights, by the end of 1982 and at five-year intervals thereafter, to report on the practical success of the section in balancing the various interests, and to make recommendations for any needed changes. With respect to audiovisual news programs, the House bill limited the scope of the distribution privilege confirmed by section 108 (f) (3) to cases where the distribution takes the form of a loan.

b. Conference Report: Conference Committee Discussion of CONTU Guidelines on Photocopying and Interlibrary Arrangements

Conference substitute

The conference substitute adopts the provisions of section 108 as amended by the House bill. In doing so, the conferees have noted two letters dated September 22, 1976, sent respectively to John L. McClellan, Chairman of the Senate Judiciary Subcommittee on Patents, Trademarks, and Copyrights, and to Robert W. Kastenmeier, Chairman of the House Judiciary Subcommittee on Courts, Civil Liberties, and the Administration of Justice. The letters, from the Chairman of the National Commission on New Technological Uses of Copyrighted Works (CONTU), Stanley H. Fuld, transmitted a document consisting of "guidelines interpreting the provision in subsection 108 (g) (2) of S. 22, as approved by the House Committee on the Judiciary." Chairman Fuld's letters explain that, following lengthy consultations with the parties concerned, the Commission adopted these guidelines as fair and workable and with the hope that the conferees on S. 22 may find that they merit inclusion in the conference report. The letters add that, although time did not permit securing signatures of the representatives of the principal library organizations or of the organizations representing publishers and authors on these guidelines, the Commission had received oral assurances from these representatives that the guidelines are acceptable to their organizations.

The conference committee understands that the guidelines are not intended as, and cannot be considered, explicit rules or directions governing any and all cases, now or in the future. It is recognized that their purpose is to provide guidance in the most commonly-encountered interlibrary photocopying situations, that they are not intended to be limiting or determinative in themselves or with respect to other situations, and that they deal with an evolving situation that will undoubtedly require their continuous reevaluation and adjustment. With these qualifications, the conference committee agrees that the guidelines are a reasonable interpretation of the proviso of section 108 (g) (2) in the most common situations to which they apply today.

c. Conference Report: Reprint of CONTU Guidelines on Photocopying and Interlibrary Arrangements

The text of the guidelines follows:

PHOTOCOPYING—INTERLIBRARY ARRANGEMENTS INTRODUCTION
Subsection 108(g)(2) of the bill deals, among other things, with limits on interlibrary arrangements for photocopying. It prohibits systematic photocopying of copyrighted materials but permits interlibrary arrangements "that do not have, as their purpose or effect,

that the library or archives receiving such copies or phonorecords for distribution does so in such aggregate quantities as to substitute for a subscription to or purchase of such work."

The National Commission on New Technological Uses of Copyrighted Works offered its good offices to the House and Senate subcommittees in bringing the interested parties together to see if agreement could be reached on what a realistic definition would be of "such aggregate quantities." The Commission consulted with the parties and suggested the interpretation which follows, on which there has been substantial agreement by the principal library, publisher, and author organizations. The Commission considers the guidelines which follow to be a workable and fair interpretation of the intent of the proviso portion of subsection 108(g)(2).

These guidelines are intended to provide guidance in the application of section 108 to the most frequently encountered interlibrary case: a library's obtaining from another library, in lieu of interlibrary loan, copies of articles from relatively recent issues of periodicals—those published within five years prior to the date of the request. The guidelines do not specify what aggregate quantity of copies of an article or articles published in a periodical, the issue date of which is more than five years prior to the date when the request for the copy thereof is made, constitutes a substitute for a subscription to such periodical. The meaning of the proviso to subsection 108(g)(2) in such case is left to future interpretation.

The point has been made that the present practice on interlibrary loans and use of photocopies in lieu of loans may be supplemented or even largely replaced by a system in which one or more agencies or institutions, public or private, exist for the specific purpose of providing a central source for photocopies. Of course, these guidelines would not apply to such a situation.

GUIDELINES FOR THE PROVISO OF SUBSECTION 108 (G)(2)
1. As used in the proviso of subsection 108 (g) (2), the words ". . . such aggregate quantities as to substitute for a subscription to or purchase of such work" shall mean:

(a) with respect to any given periodical (as opposed to any given issue of a periodical), filled requests of a library or archives (a "requesting entity") within any calendar year for a total of six or more copies of an article or articles published in such periodical within five years prior to the date of the request. These guidelines specifically shall not apply, directly or indirectly, to any request of a requesting entity for a copy or copies of an article or articles published in any issue of a periodical, the publication date of which is more than five years prior to the date when the request is made. These guidelines do not define the meaning, with respect to such a request, of ". . . such aggregate quantities as to substitute for a subscription to [such periodical]".

(b) With respect to any other material described in subsection 108 (d), (including fiction and poetry), filled requests of a requesting entity within any calendar year for a total of six or more copies or phonorecords of or from any given work (including a collective work) during the entire period when such material shall be protected by copyright.

2. In the event that a requesting entity—

(a) shall have in force or shall have entered an order for a subscription to a periodical, or

(b) has within its collection, or shall have entered an order for, a copy or phonorecord of any other copyrighted work, material from either category of which it desires to obtain by copy from another library or archives (the "supplying entity"), because the material to be copied is not reasonably available for use by the requesting entity itself, then the fulfillment of such request shall be treated as though the requesting entity made such copy from its own collection. A library or archives may request a copy or phonorecord from a supplying entity only under those circumstances where the requesting entity would have been able, under the other provisions of section 108, to supply such copy from materials in its own collection.

3. No request for a copy or phonorecord of any material to which these guidelines apply may be fulfilled by the supplying entity unless such request is accompanied by a representation by the requesting entity that the request was made in conformity with these guidelines.

4. The requesting entity shall maintain records of all requests made by it for copies or phonorecords of any materials to which these guidelines apply and shall maintain records of the fulfillment of such requests, which records shall be retained until the end of the third complete calendar year after the end of the calendar year in which the respective request shall have been made.

5. As part of the review provided for in subsection 108 (i), these guidelines shall be reviewed not later than five years from the effective date of this bill.

d. Conference Report: Discussion of "Audiovisual News Program"

The conference committee is aware that an issue has arisen as to the meaning of the phrase "audiovisual news program" in section 108(f)(3). The conferees believe that, under the provision as adopted in the conference substitute, a library or archives qualifying under section 108 (a) would be free, without regard to the archival activities of the Library of Congress or any other organization, to reproduce, on videotape or any other medium of fixation or reproduction, local, regional, or network newscasts, interviews concerning current news events, and on-the-spot coverage of news events, and to distribute a limited number of reproductions of such a program on a loan basis.

e. Conference Report: Discussion of Libraries and Archives in Profit-Making Institutions

Another point of interpretation involves the meaning of "indirect commercial advantage," as used in section 108(a)(1), in the case of libraries or archival collections within industrial, profit-making, or proprietary institutions. As long as the library or archives meets the criteria in section 108

(a) and the other requirements of the section, including the prohibitions against multiple and systematic copying in subsection (g), the conferees consider that the isolated, spontaneous making of single photocopies by a library or archives in a for-profit organization without any commercial motivation, or participation by such a library or archives in interlibrary arrangements, would come within the scope of section 108.

5. Copyright Office Regulations Under Section 108

===
The following is the text of regulations adopted by the Copyright Office to implement sections 108(d)(2) and 108(e) of the new copyright law (37 Code of Federal Regulations Sec. 201.14).
===

Section 201.14 Warnings of copyright for use by certain libraries and archives.
(a) Definitions. (1) A "Display Warning of Copyright" is a notice under paragraphs (d)(2) and
(e)(2) of section 108 of Title 17 of the United States Code as amended by Pub. L. 94-553. As
required by those sections the "Display Warning of Copyright" is to be displayed at the place
where orders for copies or phonorecords are accepted by certain libraries and archives.

(2) An "Order Warning of Copyright" is a notice under paragraphs (d) (2) and (e)(2) of section
108 of Title 17 of the United States Code as amended by Pub. L. 94-553. As required by those
sections the "Order Warning of Copyright" is to be included on printed forms supplied by
certain libraries and archives and used by their patrons for ordering copies or phonorecords.

(b) Contents. A Display Warning of Copyright and an Order Warning of Copyright shall
consist of a verbatim reproduction of the following notice, printed in such size and form and
displayed in such manner as to comply with paragraph (c) of this section:

NOTICE WARNING CONCERNING COPYRIGHT RESTRICTIONS
The copyright law of the United States (Title 17, United States Code) governs the making of
photocopies or other reproductions of copyrighted material.

Under certain conditions specified in the law, libraries and archives are authorized to furnish
a photocopy or other reproduction. One of these specified conditions is that the photocopy
or reproduction is not to be "used for any purpose other than private study, scholarship, or
research." If a user makes a request for, or later uses, a photocopy or reproduction for
purposes in excess of "fair use," that user may be liable for copyright infringement.

This institution reserves the right to refuse to accept a copying order if, in its judgment,
fulfillment of the order would involve violation of copyright law.

(c)Form and Manner of Use.

(1) A Display Warning of Copyright shall be printed on heavy paper or other durable material
in type at least 18 points in size, and shall be displayed prominently, in such manner and
location as to be clearly visible, legible, and comprehensible to a casual observer within the
immediate vicinity of the place where orders are accepted.

(2) An Order Warning of Copyright shall be printed within a box located prominently on the
order form itself, either on the front side of the form or immediately adjacent to the space
calling for the name or signature of the person using the form. The notice shall be printed in
type size no smaller than that used predominantly throughout the form, and in no case shall
the type size be smaller than 8 points. The notice shall be printed in such manner as to be
clearly legible, comprehensible, and readily apparent to a casual reader of the form.

———————————————— E. LIABILITY FOR INFRINGEMENT ————————————————

1. Text of Section 504

===
The following is a reprint of the entire text of section 504 of title 17, United States Code. The
special provisions affecting librarians and educators are in subsection (c)(2).
===

Section 504. Remedies for infringement: Damages and profits. [3]

(a) IN GENERAL.—Except as otherwise provided by this title, an infringer of copyright is liable for either—

(1) the copyright owner's actual damages and any additional profits of the infringer, as provided by subsection (b); or

(2) statutory damages, as provided by subsection (c).

(b) ACTUAL DAMAGES AND PROFITS.—The copyright owner is entitled to recover the actual damages suffered by him or her as a result of the infringement, and any profits of the infringer that are attributable to the infringement and are not taken into account in computing the actual damages. In establishing the infringer's profits, the copyright owner is required to present proof only of the infringer's gross revenue, and the infringer is required to prove his or her deductible expenses and the elements of profit attributable to factors other than the copyrighted work.

(c) STATUTORY DAMAGES.—

(1) Except as provided by clause (2) of this subsection, the copyright owner may elect, at any time before final judgment is rendered, to recover, instead of actual damages and profits, an award of statutory damages for all infringements involved in the action, with respect to any one work, for which any one infringer is liable individually, or for which any two or more infringers are liable jointly and severally, in a sum of not less than $500 or more than $20,000 as the court considers just. For the purposes of this subsection, all the parts of a compilation or derivative work constitute one work.

(2) In a case where the copyright owner sustains the burden of proving, and the court finds, that infringement was committed willfully, the court in its discretion may increase the award of statutory damages to a sum of not more than $100,000. In a case where the infringer sustains the burden of proving, and the court finds, that such infringer was not aware and had no reason to believe that his or her acts constituted an infringement of copyright, the court in its discretion may reduce the award of statutory damages to a sum of not less than $200. The court shall remit statutory damages in any case where an infringer believed and had reasonable grounds for believing that his or her use of the copyrighted work was a fair use under section 107, if the infringer was: (i) an employee or agent of a nonprofit educational institution, library, or archives acting within the scope of his or her employment who, or such institution, library, or archives itself, which infringed by reproducing the work in copies or phonorecords; or (ii) a public broadcasting entity which or a person who, as a regular part of the non-profit activities of a public broadcasting entity (as defined in subsection (g) of section 118) infringed by performing a published nondramatic literary work or by reproducing a transmission program embodying a performance of such a work.

2. Excerpts From House Report on Section 504

IN GENERAL

A cornerstone of the remedies sections and of the bill as a whole is section 504, the provision dealing with recovery of actual damages, profits, and statutory damages. The two basic aims of this section are reciprocal and correlative: (1) to give the courts specific unambiguous directions concerning monetary awards, thus avoiding the confusion and uncertainty that have marked the present law on the subject, and, at the same time, (2) to provide the courts with reasonable latitude to adjust recovery to the circumstances of the case, thus avoiding some of the artificial or overly technical awards resulting from the language of the existing statute.

Subsection (a) lays the groundwork for the more detailed provisions of the section by establishing the liability of a copyright infringer for either "the copyright owner's actual damages and any additional profits of the infringer," or statutory damages. Recovery of actual damages and profits under section 504 (b) or of statutory damages under section 504 (c) is alternative and for the copyright owner to elect; as under the present law, the plaintiff in an infringement suit is not obliged to submit proof of damages and profits and may choose to rely on the provision for minimum statutory damages. However, there is nothing in section 504 to prevent a court from taking account of evidence concerning actual damages and profits in making an award of statutory damages within the range set out in subsection (c).

Actual damages and profits

In allowing the plaintiff to recover "the actual damages suffered by him or her as a result of the infringement," plus any of the infringer's profits "that are attributable to the infringement and are not taken into account in computing the actual damages," section 504 (b) recognizes the different purposes served by awards of damages and profits. Damages are awarded to compensate the copyright owner for losses from the infringement, and profits are awarded to prevent the infringer from unfairly benefiting from a wrongful act.***

Statutory damages

Subsection (c) of section 504 makes clear that the plaintiff's election to recover statutory damages may take place at any time during the trial before the court has rendered its final judgment. The remainder of clause (1) of the subsection represents a statement of the general rates applicable to awards of statutory damages.

Clause (2) of section 504 (c) provides for exceptional cases in which the maximum award of statutory damages could be raised from $10,000 to $50,000, and in which the minimum recovery could be reduced from $250 to $100. The basic principle underlying this provision is that the courts should be given discretion to increase statutory damages in cases of willful infringement and to lower the minimum where the infringer is innocent. The language of the clause makes clear that in these situations the burden of proving willfulness rests on the copyright owner and that of proving innocence rests on the infringer, and that the court must make a finding of either willfulness or innocence in order to award the exceptional amounts.

The "innocent infringer" provision of section 504(c)(2) has been the subject of extensive discussion. The exception, which would allow reduction of minimum statutory damages to $100 where the infringer "was not aware and had no reason to believe that his or her acts constituted an infringement of copyright," is sufficient to protect against unwarranted liability in cases of occasional or isolated innocent infringement, and it offers adequate insulation to users, such as broadcasters and newspaper publishers, who are particularly vulnerable to this type of infringement suit. On the other hand, by establishing a realistic floor for liability, the provision preserves its intended deterrent effect; and it would not allow an infringer to escape simply because the plaintiff failed to disprove the defendant's claim of innocence.

In addition to the general "innocent infringer" provision clause (2) deals with the special situation of teachers, librarians, archivists, and public broadcasters, and the non-profit institutions of which they are a part. Section 504 (c)(2) provides that, where such a person or institution infringes copyrighted material in the honest belief that what they were doing constituted fair use, the court is precluded from awarding any statutory damages. It is intended that, in cases involving this provision, the burden of proof with respect to the defendant's good faith should rest on the plaintiff.

3. Excerpts From Conference Report on Section 504

==

The following excerpts are reprinted from the Report of the
Conference Committee on the new copyright law (H.R. Rep. No. 94-1733,
pages 79-80).

==

REMEDIES FOR COPYRIGHT INFRINGEMENT
Senate bill

Chapter 5 of the Senate bill dealt with civil and criminal infringement of copyright and the remedies for both. Subsection (c) of section 504 allowed statutory damages within a stated dollar range, and clause (2) of that subsection provided for situations in which the maximum could be exceeded and the minimum lowered; the court was given discretion to reduce or remit statutory damages entirely where a teacher, librarian, or archivist believed that the infringing activity constituted fair use.***
House bill

Section 504(c)(2) of the House bill required the court to remit statutory damages entirely in cases where a teacher, librarian, archivist, or public broadcaster, or the institution to which they belong, infringed in the honest belief that what they were doing constituted fair use.***
Conference substitute

The conference substitute adopts the House amendments with respect to statutory damages in section 504(c)(2)***

===
The following excerpts are reprinted from the House Report on piracy and counterfeiting
amendments   (H.R.   97-495,   pages   8-9).
===

In March 1979, Congressman Robert Kastenmeier, Chairman of the House Subcommittee
on Courts, Civil Liberties and Administration of Justice, appointed a Negotiating Committee
consisting of representatives of educational organizations, copyright proprietors, and creative
guilds and unions. The following guidelines reflect the Negotiating Committee's consensus
as to the application of "fair use" to the recording, retention, and use of television broadcast
programs for educational purposes. They specify periods of retention and use of such off-air
recordings in classrooms and similar places devoted to instruction and for homebound
instruction. The purpose of establishing these guidelines is to provide standards for both
owners and users of copyrighted television programs.

(1) The guidelines were developed to apply only to off-air recording by non-profit educational
institutions.

(2) A broadcast program may be recorded off-air simultaneously with broadcast transmission
(including simultaneous cable transmission) and retained by a non-profit educational
institution for a period not to exceed the first forty-five (45) consecutive calendar days after
date of recording. Upon conclusion of such retention period, all off-air recordings must be
erased or destroyed immediately. "Broadcast programs" are television programs transmitted
by television stations for reception by the general public without charge.

(3) Off-air recordings may be used once by individual teachers in the course of relevant
teaching activities, and repeated once only when instructional reinforcement is necessary, in
classrooms and similar places devoted to instruction within a single building, cluster, or
campus, as well as in the homes of students receiving formalized home instruction, during
the first ten (10) consecutive school days in the forty-five (45) day calendar day retention
period. "School days" are school session days—not counting weekends, holidays, vacations,
examination periods, or other scheduled interruptions—within the forty-five (45) calendar
day retention period.

(4) Off-air recordings may be made only at the request of, and used by, individual teachers,
and may not be regularly recorded in anticipation of requests. No broadcast program may be
recorded off-air more than once at the request of the same teacher, regardless of the number
of times the program may be broadcast.

(5) A limited number of copies may be reproduced from each off-air recording to meet the
legitimate needs of teachers under these guidelines. Each such additional copy shall be subject
to all provisions governing the original recording.

(6) After the first ten (10) consecutive school days, off-air recording may be used up to the
end of the forty-five (45) calendar day retention period only for teacher evaluation purposes,
i.e., to determine whether or not to include the broadcast program in the teaching curriculum,

and may not be used in the recording institution for student exhibition or any other non-evaluation purpose without authorization.

(7) Off-air recordings need not be used in their entirety, but the recorded programs may not be altered from their original content. Off-air recordings may not be physically or electronically combined or merged to constitute teaching anthologies or compilations.

(8) All copies of off-air recordings must include the copyright notice on the broadcast program as recorded.

(9) Educational institutions are expected to establish appropriate control procedures to maintain the integrity of these guidelines.

————— ENDNOTES:

[1] Corrected from Congressional Record.

[2] Editor's Note: As reprinted in the House Report, subsection A.2 of the Music Guidelines had consisted of two separate paragraphs, one dealing with multiple copies and a second dealing with single copies. In his introductory remarks during the House debates on S.22, the Chairman of the House Judiciary Subcommittee, Mr. Kastenmeier, announced that "the report, as printed, does not reflect a subsequent change in the joint guidelines which was described in a subsequent letter to me from a representative of [the signatory organizations]," and provided the revised text of subsection A.2. (122 CONG. REC. H 10875, Sept. 22, 1976). The text reprinted here is the revised text.

[3] NOTE: Section 504 was amended in subsection (c) by the Act of October 31, 1988, Pub. L. 100-568, 102 Stat. 2853, 2860.

Library of Congress
Copyright Office
101 Independence Avenue, S.E.
Washington, D.C. 20559-6000
http://www.loc.gov/copyright
September 1995 - 20,000
WEB REV: June 1998

www.ingramcontent.com/pod-product-compliance
Lightning Source LLC
Chambersburg PA
CBHW051926250726
48659CB00002B/857